Wake
Your
Successful
Self
Up

Practical Wisdom On How You Can Better Serve
Yourself and Those Around You

Felix Anderson

Wake Your Successful Self Up™

Copyright © 2016 Felix Anderson

Ordering Information:
Quantity sales. Special discounts are available on quantity purchases by corporations, associations, and others. For details, contact the publisher at the email address above.

Published by Felix Anderson

Printed in USA

First Printing, 2016

ISBN: 1539665151
ISBN-13:9781539665151

DEDICATION

To the friends, family and foes that have pushed me
to become a better version of me, I sincerely thank
you. To my children Josiah and Isaiah, I thank you
for teaching me many of the principles that will be
shared throughout this book. Josiah, when you ask
me questions like, "Daddy, what do you like most
about being a daddy?" I can honestly say that
having you and Isaiah is what I love most about
being a daddy. To my beautiful wife Tina, there
aren't enough adjectives and adverbs that can
describe what I feel for you. Your faithfulness, your
prayers and your support have helped me become
the man that I am today. All I can say is, "I LOVE
YOU," for believing in this vision and for helping
me to WAKE MY SUCCESSFUL SELF UP.

TABLE OF CONTENTS

INTRODUCTION

This book is dedicated to every person with a desire for more out of life. What began as a Freudian slip has somehow become an international trend. This book is dedicated to every person who once had a dream of becoming great but lost that dream because of someone or something. I dedicate this to you because either you or someone that's connected to you loved you enough to invest this book in your life so that you can WAKE YOUR SUCCESSFUL SELF UP!

Many times we go through life wanting to accomplish our goals only to find an element of frustration along the way. For some reaching these goals is an easy task. For others it is a struggle. Some days are better than others in that we wake up feeling like we can conquer the world. Other days we just want to place the covers of life over our heads and continue to hit that imaginary snooze button all day long. If you are in a place in life where you feel like hitting that snooze button and sleeping on your potential, this book is your manual to stay alert and stay awake so that you can continue the path of greatness.

No more sleeping on your dreams! No more sleeping on your potential! No more sleeping on your purpose! It's time for your preparation to collide with your purpose and it's time for you to WAKE YOUR SUCCESSFUL SELF UP!

Each of us was born with the desire to become great. As you read this book remember these words.

GREATNESS IS ON THE INSIDE YOU.
DO NOT ALLOW ANYONE TO TELL YOU
DIFFERENT!

WYSSU™ CREED

**I AM SUCCESSFUL BEYOND MEASURE!
I BREATHE SUCCESS, LIVE SUCCESS
BECAUSE I WAS BORN TO BE SUCCESSFUL**

**I THINK SUCCESSFUL THOUGHTS
I SPEAK SUCCESSFUL WORDS AND I MAKE
SUCCESSFUL DECISIONS
I ONLY CONNECT WITH SUCCESS MINDED
INDIVIDUALS**

**I REFUSE TO BE AVERAGE BECAUSE I
WASN'T CREATED TO BE AVERAGE.
IF I WANTED TO BE AVERAGE I COULD
HAVE STAYED IN BED
AND BECAUSE I AM AWAKE
I CHOOSE TO EMBRACE AND OPERATE IN
EXCELLENCE.**

**I CHOOSE TO WAKE MY SUCCESSFUL
SELF UP
SPIRITUALLY, MENTALLY, PHYSICALLY
AND FINANCIALLY.**

**I SPEAK TO THE CORE OF WHO I AM AND I
SAY TO MYSELF AND THOSE WHO ARE
AROUND ME....
WAKE YOUR SUCCESSFUL SELF UP!**

1

WYSSU AND APOLOGIZE

"The Best Apology is changing your behavior"
~ Tina Anderson

Wake Your Successful Self Up isn't just a slogan, it is a mindset. This mindset comes with accepting responsibility for the things that we can change and forgiving ourselves for the things that happened in our life that was and is beyond our control. In the pages to follow, you will find a list of important mindsets, and acronyms designed to prepare you for your next level along with principles that will help you maintain those mindsets.

In order for you to become a better version of you, you must first began by apologizing to yourself and accepting your own apology. As with all of my messages of hope and life, my purpose on earth is to teach you how to better serve yourself and those around you. As the old saying goes, *"Charity starts at home so before we can love others, we must first learn to love ourselves."*

Many of us have fallen out of love with our purpose, our goals and even ourselves because we have allowed someone or something from past or present to convince us otherwise. We have shared with them something that we loved only to ask for their opinion and to hear them say that they hate it.

YOU HAD A PURPOSE BEFORE THEY HAD AN OPINION.

Never allow the opinions of people not permanently connected to your future to become louder than the voice inside of you telling you to do what you love.

Now is the time for you to give birth to your dreams, your plans and your goals. It all begins with loving yourself enough to apologize to yourself for not loving yourself enough to believe in yourself. It is difficult for us to love others and do what we love if we do not love ourselves. It is difficult to love ourselves when we are harboring hate, unforgiveness, bitterness and an unspoken and unacknowledged apology that we have yet to give ourselves. I challenge you to have a genuine heart to heart conversation with the person you see every day when you look in the mirror. This perhaps may be one of the hardest conversations that you ever have because while it is easy to fool others, it is difficult to fool yourself. You know you and you can't fool YOU.

The Alignment Principle

Waking Your Successful Self Up is about learning to live again by learning to love again. This all begins with **THE ALIGNMENT PRINCIPLE**. It will help you regain focus on the person that matters most during the process of Waking Your Successful Self Up and that person is YOU! When your relationship with YOU is not in proper alignment, it opens the door for an unhealthy balance in your relationship with others.

The focus of this principle is to assist you with learning the importance of loving yourself again. If you find it difficult to be happy for others, it's not only an insult to them but also an insult to God. You are unique and there is no other human being on this planet designed and created to be like you. When you spend time loving who you are, you won't have time hating on who and what others are becoming. Loving yourself begins now with you apologizing to yourself!

THE APOLOGY

The Principle of Proper Alignment

<u>APOLOGIZE TO YOURSELF</u>

I apologize to you for not believing in you. For holding firm to the plans and goals that only you can birth into the world. I apologize to you for allowing the opinions of others to become stronger and louder than the truth about who you really are. I apologize to you for being too lazy, too stubborn, too prideful and too comfortable to step out on your dreams and following your heart. To the person that I am looking at in the mirror, I speak to you and I say to you that I apologize for not causing you to be the best version of you.

ACCEPT YOUR APOLOGY

PLACE YOUR NAME HERE

I accept your apology.

I will never again resort to becoming a watered down version of my true self.

I will hold firm to my plans and my goals and I will give birth to all that is within me that will be uplifting and edifying to mankind.

I say to you and to all of those who are in your environment...

WAKE YOUR SUCCESSFUL SELF UP

"The evidence of change isn't found on the surface of words, it's found at the foundation of your actions"

~

Wake Your Successful Self Up

2

ARE YOU R.E.A.D.Y
TO
WAKE YOUR SUCCESSFUL
SELF UP?

"No man ever reached excellence in any one art or
profession without passing through the slow and
painful process of study and preparation"
~ Horace, Ancient Roman Poet

As you embrace the journey to Wake Your
Successful Self Up, the question that you
must ask yourself is, "Am I Ready?" Desiring a
better life is not enough if we are not properly
prepared. Excellence just like your growth isn't
automatic. In order for you to experience consistent

success you cannot play by the rules. Rules have their place but they do not guarantee results. Rules can sometimes become outdated and no longer work depending on the situation or the current season of your life. A rule can box you in and cause you to become stagnant preventing you from taking risks and expanding your mindset. Principles on the other hand guarantee results. What goes up must come down, you will reap what you sow are just a few.

However, none of us have ever truly reaped everything that we have sown, because there were some bad seeds that we planted that never manifested. Many of us have sown some things in our lives, that had it not been for grace, the bad seeds sown would have had us in a different place in life at this very moment. Despite all of this, the principle of seed, time and harvest still remains and you must have principles planted in your mind if you want to grow. Seeds produce after its own kind. For example, if you want tomatoes you plant tomatoes but if you want money you are going to have to plant some money. You cannot expect to receive tomatoes planting watermelon seeds as that would be foolish. So it is in the area of time, energy, finances and all other areas of life. While it is true that seeds produce after its own kind, just because you give something in one way does not mean that it will necessarily come back in the same measure. If we want to obtain knowledge from someone who is skillful in any area of life, you give them money in exchange for goods.

THE PLANTING PRINCIPLE

The primary focus of the planting principle is to give with the expectation of seeing a return on that which you have invested. Some people may give to you and say, I don't want anything in return when in fact they do. They may not want something directly from you, but they want to see the pain, heartache, frown and hardship you're experiencing to turn around for the better and that's why they give to you. You may be prompted to give to a charitable organization for tax purposes and during the journey of life, you may need wisdom and guidance. You may find yourself receiving that very wisdom and guidance from someone who usually charges for the information shared. The money you planted in that charitable organization did not come back in the immediate form of money, but it came back in a different form that saved you money yet provided you insight on how you can possibly make more money. Giving is a principle that is the cornerstone for prosperity in all areas of your life. To expect a harvest without first planting a seed of any kind is an illusion at its finest.

> **Don't expect the harvest of the rich if you are going to keep practicing the habits of the poor.**

PRINCIPLE OF PERSPECTIVE

The principle of perspective is the foundation to Waking Your Successful Self Up. You must make the daily decision to not live your life based on rules. You must live your life based on principles, because rules change but principles do not. You must make the decision to plant only good thoughts in your head about yourself and those around you so that you can see those things from a different set of lenses. Your perspective on life must constantly evolve to the place where you begin to see beyond what you see. Learning to view your situation not for what it is but viewing it for what it could or can be is vital. My mother use to say, "I'm just calling it like I see", but as I have matured in life, I have realized that many times you can't afford to call things like you see. Many times how you see it may not be favorable for you, which is why you must change your perspective so you can change your position.

If you are speaking your current situation, you will forever remain in that current situation. Change your perspective because your sight can distort your vision if you are not focused. It's not always how you see the things around you that matter. Many times it's what you see in the things that are happening around you that matter. Our pain can sometimes push us into our purpose, but our perspective will help us see our way out of it. Always speak the end from the beginning and do not call it like you see it, call it like you want to see it.

> **"It's easy to have principles when you're rich. The important thing is to have principles when you're poor." ~ Ray Kroc**

PRINCIPLE OF PRUNING

Sometimes the best decision you will ever make will be the toughest. These tough decisions sometimes include eliminating things we like and things we love that are no longer beneficial to our pattern of growth. Some of the stress you are experiencing will be eliminated once you develop and implement a solidified strategy of pruning. The principle of pruning is the process of looking at things from an either/or perspective. Either the people and things connected to you are beneficial or they are detrimental. Either they are causing you to grow or fail. When it comes to Waking Your

Successful Self Up, either you are going to do it or you are not. Every day won't be easy but when your mind is made up, it brings clarity to your purpose even when your present predicament may not look promising. Like dead leaves on a plant, in order for you to receive the proper nourishment that you need to succeed, you must make the tough decision to make some cuts. Understand that you can't grow until you let some things and some people go.

Everyone can't be attached to you during your entire journey. Sometimes you have to go alone and sometimes you have to grow alone. Don't depend on people to always go and grow with you. Your wilderness will always precede your wonderland and that is why what you carry and who you carry with you along the journey is vital. Carrying people that were only designed to be connected to you for a short period of time can contaminate your purpose. It has no bearing on whether or not they are nice, but it has everything to do with whether or not they are needed in this season of your life.

The cultivation of your gift cost you too much for it to be contaminated by foolishness. Pay attention only to what needs attention and ignore everything else so that you can have the power to cut the non-essentials off so you can grow and go to another level. Sometimes there will be no need to eliminate things out of your life if you have high character. If you keep your character high, eventually that which is not beneficial to your life will leave because darkness can't survive in light. Keep in mind that unnecessary stress comes from holding on to people, places and things you have simply outgrown and have been instructed to release from your life. Like clothes, there are some relationships you just simply outgrow. It doesn't mean that something is wrong with them, it's just that you've grown and they no longer fit.

> **"Your inability to cut things off will overwhelm you and because you can't let go of it, it will kill you" ~ Bishop T.D. Jakes**

Don't go back and don't look back. Don't try to force fit what is no longer designed to fit. Don't try to rekindle a relationship or situation that God has specifically told you to release. WAKE YOUR SUCCESSFUL SELF UP and let them go and let it go so that you can experience a fresh start. Today is the day for you to Make the List and Make the Cuts of everything stunting your growth.

> **"I'm married to principles, but I'm never married to methods. Methods change, but principles are constant" ~ Oral Roberts**

2-7-8 GET READY TO GROW

This introductory chapter is preparation for your Wake Your Successful Self Up journey. At the end of this chapter you will find the 278 Principle that will serve as your guide for facilitating your growth. The principle of planting, changing your perspective and pruning are all designed to get you ready to grow. Growth comes with pain, sacrifice, criticism and discomfort. A tree doesn't complain about the weather because it is so focused on growing. The storm of life may have hit you but you are still breathing and you are still alive.

Celebrate your discomfort because it is a sign that you are growing. Acknowledge the discomfort when it happens because unaddressed hurt grows up to be deep rooted anger and anger turns into bitterness. Pluck that up from the root immediately and never allow bitterness to block your blessings. There will be times during your growth that you will experience delays. Situations that look like delays are actually opportunities for you to grow, get experience and meet people purposed to help you later in life. Your growth and progress will always face opposition but you cannot afford to give up.

If You Want To Grow, Remain Teachable.

Understand that when you grow up inwardly, you GROW UP outwardly and there are certain things that should never be attached to your name or your character. You cannot have a grown gift and childish character and expect to be successful. When you are provided the opportunity to grow, be cognizant of your own pettiness because being petty will prevent your launch. Not only do you have to be aware of your pettiness, but you must also eliminate and be aware of the pettiness around you.

If the people close to you aren't growing relationally, spiritually, emotionally or professionally, neither will you. When people really care about you growing, they will say something to you about the areas of your life that you need to address. If they sit in silence only to watch you fail you need to be on high alert because snakes don't talk. When you grow up you won't waste your time trying to keep up simply because you are your own competition. Other trees don't concern themselves with other trees because their focus is staying rooted in where they are planted. As you begin to grow your gift will indeed make room for you but if you are not in a place where your gift can grow, you will suffocate.

Be strong enough to let go and smart enough to move on. Sometimes staying connected too long can stunt your growth. Your growth should be intentional with no apologies attached and the time to start growing is NOW!!!

> **Learn how to listen to people who have been where you haven't. The stories of their path can stop you from experiencing unnecessary pain. Always remain teachable.**

THE 278 MOVEMENT

IS A CHALLENGE TO ANYONE SEEKING TO IMPROVE ACCOUNTABILITY, TIME MANAGEMENT AND A NEW MINDSET. WHY THE NUMBERS 278? HERE IS WHY...

(1) THE BIBLE ASKS A QUESTION IN AMOS 3:3 AND I QUOTE "HOW CAN TWO WALK TOGETHER EXCEPT THEY AGREE?" THERE MUST BE AN AGREEMENT BETWEEN YOU AND WHOEVER YOU PARTNER WITH SPIRITUALLY, MENTALLY, PROFESSIONALLY, AND EMOTIONALLY IN ORDER FOR PROSPERITY TO TAKE PLACE.

(2) 7 IS THE NUMBER OF COMPLETION AND I CHALLENGE YOU TO WRITE DOWN (7) THINGS YOU WANT TO SEE HAPPEN IN THE NEXT 6 MONTHS. PRAY ABOUT IT, PEN IT, PROCLAIM IT AND MAKE PREPARATIONS FOR IT TO HAPPEN!!!

(3) 8 IS THE NUMBER OF NEW BEGINNINGS. BEFORE YOU CAN EXPERIENCE NEW BEGINNINGS, HERE ARE THE THINGS YOU MUST CHECK OFF YOUR LIST.

☐ FIND SOMEONE THAT WILL AGREE WITH HELPING YOU PROSPER MENTALLY, SPIRITUALLY, PHYSICALLY AND EMOTIONALLY.

☐ PRAY ABOUT IT, PEN IT, PROCLAIM IT AND PREPARE FOR IT THEN YOU WILL...

☐ BE READY FOR YOUR NEW BEGINNINGS!!!

> **"Change your circumstances through the words you speak. You may have fallen on your face but you have to get up" ~ Kenya Parks**

If you can't make things better with your words, don't open your mouth and make them worse with your words.

~

Wake Your Successful Self Up

3

RESET YOUR MIND

"Your world is a living expression of how you are
using and have used your mind"
~ Earl Nightingale

Now that you are ready and committed to WAKING YOUR SUCCESSFUL SELF UP, resetting your mindset for the level of greatness you are about to enter is important. Once your mindset changes, everything on the outside will change along with it. Trying to enter a new arena of your life with an old mindset will lead you right back into the problems you are presently facing so a change has to occur. You must always have a first rate mindset, always. so anything or anyone that tells you different is a liar. Understand that when you have a mindset to be first, you must be prepared to be criticized by people who have a mindset to be last. As you make the change in your mindset, it is extremely important that you stay positive at all times.

Never beat yourself up for what you are doing wrong or old habits that you may fall back into. Always focus on lessons learned and build yourself up for the things you are doing right even though you may not always get it right. Change isn't always instant and sometimes it takes time, it takes consistency, it takes patience but most of all it takes the right mindset to maintain it. Consistency makes the hard things in life easy and consistency is the key to your breakthrough.

YOU DON'T HAVE PROBLEMS

I'm a firm believer that what you verbalize is what you will visualize and what you visualize is what you will verbalize. When you Reset Your

Mindset, you began to see things from a positive perspective as opposed to a negative one. For years I called the challenges I had in life problems when in fact they were not problems at all. They were and are what I now refer to as opportunities.

When I realized this, I immediately did a hard reset mentally and verbally. You see, we don't have problems, we have opportunities. The thing you're having a challenge with solving isn't a problem. It's an opportunity for you to tap into your creative conscious to learn and grow so that it can better serve you and others. A problem is only a problem when a lack of patience is present. A problem is only a problem if you see it as a problem, but the problem is that most people don't have the patience to wait on the solution and that is when it can be perceived as a problem.

Reset your mindset and realize that you don't have problems, you have opportunities.

Put a plan in place so that you can pursue your purpose and put people in their place so that they don't poison your purpose.

~

Wake Your Successful Self Up

4

THE
PRE-ORDERED
MINDSET

"Develop a clear vision of your destination.
Disengage from activities and people not headed
in that direction. Connect with others who are
already at your desired destination."
~ Dr. Samuel Chand

The Pre-Ordered Mindset is about focusing on and practicing the law of vision. The law of vision simply states that if you can't see it, you can't have it. As mentioned earlier, what you visualize is what you will verbalize and what you verbalize is what you visualize. Where you see yourself and how you see yourself will always be where you see yourself and how you see yourself. For this very reason, you should only speak what you want to see manifest in your life and understand the power of your words. It can be tempting to call things like you see them, but what you don't see is much more real than what you see.

Boxes don't exist to open minded people and the Pre-Ordered Mindset is about you opening yourself up to the greatness that lies within. It is being able to invest in something that you can't tangibly touch at the moment because you anticipate its arrival even though it has not arrived. You cannot arrive somewhere physically unless you first arrive there mentally. The more you become sensitive to that which is not visible, it will appear as if it were. Believe it or not, every decision is a spiritual decision that transcends into the natural. Can you see where you are supposed to be?

STUDY THE BEST

You must see yourself as being successful and you must become a student of those who are successful and those who are masters of their craft.

The Pre-Ordered Mindset is about visualizing the success that the masters have modeled so that you mimic it in a manner that is tailored to your personal gifts and talent. This was best displayed by Kobe Bryant as he studied and mastered the moves of Michael Jordan. Kobe mastered Michael's mannerisms and his style of play, but the thing that set him apart from all those that tried this before was his will to succeed and his mindset to be the best. Sometimes your Pre-Ordered Mindset will drive you to accomplish that which has never been done before. This mindset will not only change you but it will create awareness to change and make everything within you and around you better.

Lewis Gordon Pugh, the first human to complete a long distance swim at the Geographic North Pole in nothing more than a Speedo, cap and goggles, is a great example of this. By swimming in a region that was once completely covered in ice, Lewis showed the world that climate change is happening and we have the power to stop it. Pugh's quote, "There is nothing more powerful than a made up mind," has been a source of motivation for me the moment I first heard it.

Once you truly make the decision to WAKE YOUR SUCCESSFUL SELF UP, nothing or no one can reverse that decision. Prepare your mind as if you have already performed and accomplished the goal you desire. If you are serious about reaching your place called there, you should be equally as serious about putting in the work to make it happen. This work begins with your thoughts and you must think excellence at all times. Pre-Order your mind as if you have reached your destination instead of acting like you haven't started preparing for the journey. Remember, that if you can't see what you desire then you can't have it. What's stopping you from achieving your dreams and your goals? What's stopping you from being the best version of you that you can be? Like Lewis Gordon Pugh, it's time for you to make up your mind to do what has never been done before by thinking on a level that you have never thought before.

"People are comfortable with you as long as you stay in seed form. As soon as you start growing into what you're suppose to be, they have a problem with you."

~

Joshua P. Smith

5

WYSSU AND
KNOW YOUR WORTH

"Make sure that you know your value because trust me, the people who try to take advantage of you, already know your worth" ~ Maranda Joiner

Wake up and know your worth. These five words are probably the most important words you will read in this book. These words determine not only how you perceive yourself but how others perceive you as well. These words are the very reason many find themselves in a ball of frustration daily simply because they know they are more valuable than the return on investment that the job, the relationship or the situation they are in is giving in return. In my conversations with individuals from all walks of life, the common denominator is that every person on this earth desires to be valued. The issues that are often at the forefront is fighting through the words of people that didn't know our value. If you do not place a value on your time, the things you create and your love, then the people that you encounter will not feel obligated to raise your value. Understand that you are valuable and it's up to you to act accordingly. When you know your worth you don't compromise so don't become emotionally bankrupt by investing your time, energy and money into people who don't value you. **Never compromise your morals and values for people who don't have either.**

CARRY YOURSELF WELL

How you speak matters, how you dress matters and how you carry yourself matters in every aspect of life. **No matter what it is or who it is, there must be a level of attraction before there can ever be a level of attachment**. People are either drawn to you by the energy that is presented in your personality or your presentation or they are repelled by it. I remember walking into an establishment once and a lady walked over to me and said, "Sir, I don't know what you do, but I know you are good at it. I can tell by the way you dress and speak. You just stand out." When she said these words, I immediately began to think about how many people say the words, "I don't care what other people think."

While we shouldn't become overly consumed with the thoughts of others toward us, we should at least take some thought to the thoughts that they have toward us. Those thoughts are simply a reflection of our inner value that is displayed outwardly when you enter an environment. Your attitude should shift the ambiance of every environment you enter for the better. People should be drawn to the love and positivity that radiates from the inward love you have for yourself deep within.

WAKE YOUR SUCCESSFUL SELF UP and SHIFT YOUR ATMOSPHERE WITH POSITIVE ENERGY AND LOVE.

Nothing is more important than knowing your value because everything comes into perspective when you do. It is practically the best thing you can ever do for yourself on earth. You have the capability to change the world, it is in you and you should not allow anything to get in your way of having the great life you were destined to have. Realize that you should be the best supporter you have in life so be your own cheerleader. Stop waiting on the perfect moment to arrive because the time is now.

We see desolation and negativity all around us daily and there could never have been a better time to be the game changer you truly are deep down with more focus, determination and motivation you could ever get. Until you value yourself, you would not value your gifts and talents or do anything meaningful with them.

DEFINE YOURSELF

You need to define yourself, value it and everything else would fall into its rightful place. You are very important and the best part is that your value increases each day you realize it. Realize that everything about you matters and you cannot allow people to place labels on you when they do not know the value of what is inside of you. Everything around you and in you will come to life when you begin to speak words of life into your life. I want to begin the process of helping you define who you are. You are royalty, you are beautiful and you are excellence personified. Be happy and comfortable with who you are and never make the mistake of comparing yourself to other people.

> **If you want to grow, you must learn to appreciate yourself well.**

DO NOT GIVE UP ON YOURSELF

Your achievements can only get you as far as the door; it is your true value that keeps you in the room. Always take into account, the unique qualities that make you and appreciate them. Always remember that how you think, talk and represent yourself could emphasize or reduce your value. Focus on your talents, skills and strengths with a goal to building them up.

ALWAYS GIVE YOURSELF PEP TALKS

Whenever you feel like bolting out the door, take a deep breath and find a mirror and speak only that which is positive. Say only those things that are great about yourself and those around you. Every morning I look myself in the eyes through the mirror and say, **"Never become insulted by the fact that you could be better at what you do."** These same words will help you boost your self-confidence and help you to realize that you do matter. The weight of being a strong and whole person rests on you and not the opinions of others.

Realize that you were created to be creative and to be great. Never equate your value with the societal scale or standards of value. People will always have opinions of what they think of you, but it is what you think of yourself that matters most. You are worth far more than you can image. You are a unique and wonderful person who has the power to change the world.

> **Respect yourself enough to know that you deserve better than toxic jobs, friendships and relationships that do not add value to your life in any measure.**

Aspire to greater things and respect yourself enough to walk away from anything that devalues you or makes you lose your happiness. Make daily efforts to constantly and consistently value yourself and not rely on others to define your worth. How you value yourself affects every area of your life either positively or negatively.

WYSSU
~ Wisdom List ~

Devote your time to only things worthy of your appreciation, time, energy and sacrifice.

You are your own best friend. How you feel about yourself is inversely proportional to how you treat yourself.

No matter how many wrongs and mistakes you have made in your life, you are still a person worthy of the best things life has to offer.

Never feel hopeless and helpless about yourself. You are alive for a reason.

Never get distracted by your weakness. Everyone has their flaws, own up to yours and rock it well. Do not let it drag you down.

Learn to love your weirdness and eccentricities so you can become the best version of yourself.

Take a magnifying glass on your life through your mind and focus on the best parts.

Stop selling yourself short and instead choose to overvalue what you are and undervalue what you are not.

WYSSU
~ Wisdom Affirmations ~

Whatever I do makes a difference,
so I will act like it.

No matter what I do, someone somewhere is
waiting on me to do the right thing.

I am responsible for the quality of my life.

I am a bundle of possibilities and I will make the
best of it.

My value lies in being true to myself.

True value is not measured by how much success I
have achieved or how much money I have; it is who
I am when these things are stripped away.

My life has a purpose and a plan no matter my
background, age, experience or gender.

My value lies in how effectively I live my life and I
choose to….

**WAKE MY SUCCESSFUL SELF UP AND
KNOW MY WORTH.**

<u>LIST 7 VALUABLE THINGS</u>

<u>ABOUT YOURSELF</u>

1. _____

2. _____

3. _____

4. _____

5. _____

6. _____

7. _____

If Jesus was without honor in his hometown, why are you so bent out of shape because you're not accepted by some of the people in yours? Just because you live in an area does not mean you are called to it. Do not let a local mindset make you miss your global assignment.

~

Wake Your Successful Self Up

6

WYSSU AND KNOW YOUR PURPOSE

"I can't sleep because my purpose has my sleep pattern all off" ~ Darnell Nolin

We all have a purpose in life and the purpose of our purpose is to bring us into a greater level of communication not only with ourselves but with the One that created us and to serve others. Our purpose is that thing that keeps us in a place of peace and fulfillment. Purpose is why you were born and vision is when you start seeing it. Your purpose is that one thing that you can't go a day without thinking about. It is also that one thing

51

that will have your sleep pattern all off because you are always up thinking about giving birth to it. When we are not in our purpose we find ourselves in an uncomfortable place and a place of frustration. Your purpose is that one thing in life that you must be absolutely sure of if you want to experience true peace in your life. Notice that I didn't mention happiness, because there are times during the journey of you fulfilling your purpose that you will not be happy simply because your purpose will have you doing things outside of your comfort zone. Your comfort zone is a safe place to rest and hide but nothing grows there. If you want to advance in life, you're going to have to face adversity and step outside of the familiar and comfort. Your comfort zone is the incubator to laziness and laziness is a byproduct of not knowing your purpose.

> **"I can't relate to lazy people. We don't speak the same language. I don't understand you. I don't want to understand you." ~ Kobe Bryant**

Many of us are living a mundane life that has no meaning or purpose attached to it. While we aspire to live an inspired life where we are living each day with a purpose and the zeal to get up and live for the future, it is not usually so. So how does one get to live an inspired life and become a direct or indirect inspiration to others?

REALIZE YOUR PURPOSE IN LIFE

One thing that we fail to do is to know our purpose and reason for existence. Everyone has a purpose in life but only those who have the heart and mind to listen are able to realize their purpose and put it into use. It is imperative that you understand the purpose of your life and plan on putting it to action. Do not get caught up in doing what others think you should be doing and find yourself miserable. Many have occupations they are gifted at doing but they are not happy because they are not walking in their purpose. The most common mistake people make is comparing their process of advancement to others. Just because you are not doing what people think you should be doing does not mean you are not walking in your purpose. Don't become discouraged and think that your purpose is paralyzed because you don't see any movement. Always remember that your purpose is like a seed. It's designed to be planted deep within you so that it can produce. As with the seed, you may not see the fruit of your purpose when you are beginning your process, but do know that you will eventually produce if you persevere. Sometimes your purpose does not align with who you are and where you are in life right now but rather whom you will be and where you're purposed to be after the process is complete. Knowing your purpose does two things in particular. It will make room for you and it leaves no room for you to be jealous of others flowing in theirs.

THINK POSITIVE

A positive mind is of utmost importance for an inspired life and to be an inspiration to others. If you think positive, your actions that follow your thinking are bound to be positive. This is the basis

of a universal law called the "Law of Attraction"
and can be applied to your day activities. When you
think positive thoughts you will draw positive
people and positive experiences. By living a life
filled with positive thinking, you can be an
inspiration to yourself and to others around you. So
keep your head up and know that your purpose is
greater than those bad decisions that you made. God
is a restorer and forgiver. Don't let people keep
throwing in your face that which God has forgotten
(Isaiah 43:25). The God that has given you purpose
is greater than those coming against your purpose.
Focus on Him and not them. Keep in mind that
when you know your purpose and who you are,
those that are insecure within themselves will
become intimidated by your presence alone. **Some
people around you will look at your purpose and
say "You Can't" until they can benefit from the
fact that you did.** You cannot allow this to prevent
you from staying planted in your place of growth so
that you can fulfill your purpose. Keep working
hard even when your present position does not

match your place of purpose. Know that you are purposed for greatness and allow that to be your driving force. You do not have to be perfect to fulfill your purpose so don't waste time pretending like you have it all together. None of us do. Understand that people don't need you for your perfection; they need you for your purpose.

MOTIVATION FROM MENTORS

Everyone in life should have a mentor that they can look up to for inspiration and influence. While it is not essential to live your life based on their whims and wants, your life can take new shape if you are taking inspiration from their lives by putting it to use in carrying on with your life. **Become a student of someone who has mastered the area in which you are attempting to enter.** Find someone that will help guide you during the times in your life when you do not have clear direction. Avoid unnecessary pitfalls and detours from others who have already paved a path.

READ MOTIVATIONAL MATERIAL

You have a lot of hidden talent in you. It is only when your spirit, your mind and your body are trained that you will realize that this talent lies within you. Only when you tap into this potential that you can fully comprehend what it is that you can achieve in life. In order to reach this state of mind, you need to receive passable inspiration. We will speak about this in detail within the TTD Principle that I will share later. One method to do this is to read or listen to motivational material that can guide you to the path that you have been seeking.

ACTION PLAN

No thought process can be success unless you follow it up with an action plan and the necessary action. Unless your thoughts are put in motion, there is no value to it. So, in order to live an inspired life and be an inspiration to others around you, you need to not only think about how you are going to live, but also follow it up with the appropriate action. By doing so you are living your life to the fullest potential and living an inspired life being an inspiration to yourself as well as to those around you. As human beings we have an instinctive drive to evolve, improve, and innovate, to make things faster, smarter, easier, better, and more sustainable; and with technology we are exponentially expanding the scope of what is possible. But even as new opportunities arise, many people find their old jobs obsolete or changing and their skill sets ready for an overhaul.

Now, more than ever, it is essential to be clear about what is most important to you and how you choose to express your purpose through your life's work. Many people identify with their occupation. One of the most common things asked when people meet for the first time is: "What do you do?" So as careers shift, it can influence our self-perception. Work is a way to live your purpose and contribute to society. When a seemingly solid foundation of a career shifts, it can often lead to serious self-reflection or even a temporary feeling of loss.

It is wise to begin asking timeless questions about your purpose and your mission. What is my purpose? Why am I here? How will I fulfill my destiny? When you find your purpose, your livelihood and sense of self isn't tied to a particular job or position. This is freedom: when your thoughts, words and actions are aligned with your purpose and you live from a space of inner harmony. The most appropriate opportunities will reveal themselves.

ACCESS WISDOM THROUGH STILLNESS

How do you find your purpose and evolve yourself - not only to rise with rapid technological advances and a shifting economy, but also to direct the course of progress toward your vision for the future? How will you align your thoughts, words and actions to manifest your heart's desire? How will you develop your own inner being so that in any environment you recognize, articulate and live your purpose while expressing your talents in a way that creates life-affirming value for others and prosperity for you? You will find your purpose when you make conscious choices based on what is essential and what is of your essence. Your essence is who you are and who you choose to be. You access this wisdom through stillness. Stillness is where you find the insight to know yourself, love your life, and live your purpose. Your intuitive wisdom grows and your purpose becomes clear as you honor, welcome, and allow stillness to be the nucleus of every thought, word, and deed. You can also find your purpose by paying attention to what you love doing. The things which bring you joy are clues to your purpose.

PURPOSE QUESTIONS TO PONDER

What are you really good at?

What do you do that makes you get lost in time?

What is a natural action for you?

If you could give anything to people, what would it be?

WHAT WILL HAPPEN IF YOU DON'T FIND YOUR PURPOSE?

If you are not clear on your purpose, you will react to other people's demands. You may move towards what you deem pleasurable and move away from what you consider painful, but often your purpose is found in painful moments. Without your purpose to guide the way, it's easy to get disoriented and sucked into other people's agenda's, often without realizing it, which may or may not be in alignment with what you really want. This experience is like being swept away by a cyclone, thrown around by the winds and currents. It's disorienting and makes life harder because it's a struggle to maintain balance.

Finding your purpose is like being in the eye of the storm. It allows you to harness the wild energy, direct it, and actively chart a course. When you center yourself and live your purpose, nothing outside of you has power over you. Instead, you ride it like a wave. You choose how to perceive, and give empowering meaning to your experiences.

To find your purpose, ask yourself, "Who Am I?
You have the power to reinvent outdated self-perceptions that no longer serve your magnificence, bringing the essence of who you are into your life's work. You can choose work based not only on what you do, but rather, on who you are. Instead of defining your work by position, tasks and responsibilities, you can describe your roles by the creative contribution you offer and the fulfillment you experience from bringing value to others and our world. Work becomes an extension of spirit and then an expression of your talents; it's what you're passionate about - what you love to do, rather than what you have to do. Everyone has a gift inside, just waiting for the appropriate conditions to shine, some people along the way have been taught to compromise dreams and conform to "reality." Reality can be hard and life is ever changing. The seemingly impossible is absolutely possible with the right concoction of creativity, innovation, heart, clarity of vision and commitment.

When you follow your inner guidance and allow your passion and imagination to flow uncensored, you will be led to find your purpose and fulfill your mission. On the road to fulfilling the mission of your finding your purpose, there will be people that will insult your intelligence; there will be those that prey on you instead of praying for you.

---

5 Ways To Protect Your Purpose

(1) Use discernment at all times and know that the hidden motives of those seeking to do you wrong will always be revealed.

(2) Realize that Everybody IS NOT your friend.

(3) Understand that some people will ask you questions not because they are interested in supporting you but they will ask to see if you will open up your mouth and share where your strength lie so they can find ways to sabotage you.

(4) Selectively share your vision...People will SEE it when they SEE it.

(5) Do your research and above all READ the FINE PRINT so people won't rip you off!!! What people are saying isn't what should concern you; it's what they don't say that you need to pay attention to.

"I am a scholar of life. Every night before I go to sleep, I analyze every detail of what I did that day. I evaluate things and people, which helps me avoid mistakes."

~

Compay Segundo

7

BECOME YOUR OWN
COMPETITION

"If you spend all of your time addressing your
critics, you will become critical yourself"
~Roderick Richardson

Everyone on earth has a story that has shaped
him or her into the person they are today.
Both the positive and negative influences have
molded our thought process to either love or to hate,
to hold grudges or to forgive. Our thought processes
are the very thing that determines whether or not we
will let the words of others cause us to fail or fuel us
to succeed. Negative words never mattered much to

me because in my mind, what others said to me or about me really didn't matter. I was often told that I had a bad attitude growing up but for me it was a purposeful rebuttal when people told me what I couldn't do. I never believed the negative words others said about me to be true because I knew deep down inside that I was purposed for greatness. I used to have the mindset that if someone told me I couldn't accomplish something, I would stay up for days until I proved them wrong.

As I matured, I later learned that not only is it unwise to try and prove your critics wrong, but I found out that it is a waste of time because you are your own competition. I have also learned to become a student of those that are at the top of their game and analyze how they handle criticism. Many, like arguably the greatest basketball player of all time Michael Jordan, are fuel by criticism and were told that they weren't good enough. His example has taught me to never let the words of critics stop you from conquering.

The crowd will always be full of spectators and critics but only those who really understand what you've been through to get to where you are will be genuinely happy for you. Until you learn how to celebrate others and their success, you will never experience it and so I'm here to encourage you to keep playing. No matter how many times you have been knocked down or how many times you have seemingly lost, KEEP PLAYING!

Whether you have a good day, bad day, good game or bad game, your critics will be present. Keep in mind that the people who are the loudest and most critical are the people in the stands and they aren't playing at all. History doesn't pen critics, only champions and YOU ARE A CHAMPION! If God is Big and Bad enough to shut the mouth of lions for Daniel when he was thrown in the lion's den (Daniel 6: 16-22 NASB), then surely He is Big and Bad enough to shut the mouth of your critics.

Don't waste time fighting and arguing with people that are nowhere close to being on your level. That's wasted energy you could be using on being productive.

> **WAKE YOUR SUCCESSFUL SELF UP AND DO NOT be deceived. Everyone that is smiling at you is not happy for you.**

WYSSU
~ Wisdom List ~

Pay more attention to developing your craft than the distractions and drama of your critics.

When people outside of your inner circle approach you with statements like "I Heard or Someone Said"...
Keep in mind that people hear many things and often what they want to hear. So when you have in house issues, keep it behind those doors and close to your chest.

Never let the words of an unaccomplished critic stop you from accomplishing your goals.

Never let what people are saying about you stop you from doing what needs to be done. The critics are in the crowd for a reason.

You silence your critics through the voice of your actions.

Don't let a spectator stop you from being spectacular.

95% of the people criticizing what you do can't do what you do. The other 4% are jealous that they are not you and the 1% that really matter are either supporting you or too busy minding their own business to notice you. Don't get discouraged by what people say because your critics are always in the crowd.

~

Wake Your Successful Self Up

8

LEARN HOW TO THINK FOR YOURSELF

"If you care about what people think about you, you will end up being their slave. Reject and pull your own rope." ~ Aulio Ice

One of the greatest things you can ever be delivered from is public opinion. Elevating your thinking and your capacity to think and learn how to think for yourself is essential during this process. All too often I see people live their lives through the lenses and by the script that others have set before them. While it is great to receive wisdom and advice from others, it is also wise to be careful not to let their advice or opinion override your own personal truth and inner convictions.

71

Be careful of receiving advice from people who always preface their statements with "If I were you, I would…." That is a subtle sign of manipulation and someone trying to capitalize off of your mistakes.

Challenge yourself to follow the inner peace within when advice is given. If you receive wisdom and what you hear does not sit well with you, it could mean several things. The first thing that this could mean is that you may not be in a good place spiritually, physically or emotionally to receive the advice that was provided. To properly receive sound wisdom, you must be in a place of balance in your life. Otherwise you will either take offense to what is being said, how it's being said or who is saying it.

In my book, *Service That Makes A Statement*, I outline this in what I call The Package. I have found that in order to receive wisdom properly, you have to identity what I like to call the 3 M's. The first of these three is **THE MAN.** When I speak of man, this is not gender specific but in relation to mankind as a whole. When advice is provided to you, you must consider the source and ask yourself, is this person qualified to teach or share the information they are providing? This is important because it is difficult for one to teach success if they are not successful or have not experienced a level of success at some point in life.

Many people can share wisdom from a place of experience and in these instances; it is always wise to listen no matter where you are in your spiritual, physical or emotional state. Be careful who you receive counsel from when you're getting ready to do battle in life regardless of their position on earth. Not only is it important to check your own motives when pursuing counsel, but also it is equally important to check the motives of those providing the counsel. Sometimes people have their own agenda about your life and what they suggest you do isn't what you are purposed to do. The rules and attire for the engagements of life may change, but the principles for the engagements of life never change. Stay on high alert for the "If I were you, I would put on this or I would do that" people. Even though they may mean well, it may not be the purpose for your life.

The second thing to consider is **THE MESSAGE**. During my life and in moments of leadership and encounters with leaders, I have learned that bondage can occur in our thinking when asking for everyone's opinion. Many times we become slaves to what others think of us and more often than that, we are slaves to our own way of thinking. What you think of yourself and how you think is a major factor in whether or not you will be successful. Many employees become frustrated when they are not provided the freedom to think for themselves. They encounter supervisors, bosses and managers that provide little room for creativity and freedom to provide insight on a matter. A leader can suppress the creativity of those following him/her by not allowing them to think for themselves and bring a fresh perspective to the table. Many of these same leaders become frustrated when those they are leading do not think for themselves causing the leader to become more of a parent than a leader. Frustration exists on both ends because those being lead are not able to be creative with their thought process and those doing the leading are not seeing creative results.

This can be resolved by using the third M, which is **THE METHOD**. Since we are created in God's image and He is our creator, we were created to create. Wisdom says that we are to use the same methods God used in the beginning when He created us. Genesis 1:26-27 says "Then God said let Us make man in Our image, according to our likeness; and let them have rule over the fish of the sea and over the birds of the sky and over the cattle and over all the earth, and over every creeping thing that creeps on earth. God created man in His own image, in the image of God He created him; male and female He created them." These scriptures reveal several things. Here we see an example of God the Creator asking for assistance when He says, "Let Us make man." This is a great example of what happens when creativity and collaboration takes place. While we can never get married to methods, we must be willing to embrace the methods of others to ensure that the message we are attempting to deliver is conveyed properly. Behind every great invention, every great idea, every great mission, there is The Man, The Message and The Method. All three must be in harmony in order for them all to work effectively. If people like the man and the message but hate the method, they will not be receptive. If people like the method and the message but do not like the man, they will not be receptive. This works in all cases as it relates to employing these methods. This is why it is important that you begin to think for yourself and embrace your own unique creativity so that you can better assist those to whom you have been assigned.

T - Think for yourself. Your life will not get better until your thoughts get better. It's great to receive advice and wisdom from others, but it is equally important that you look deep within and understand that you are a creative being that has the ability to THINK for yourself.

Never allow anyone to make decisions for you that only you will have to at some point live with.

H - **Hold your peace** and guard the thoughts of your heart. Every thought that enters into your mind is not to be voiced. Everything about you and what you are hoping to accomplish in life is not designed and meant to be shared with everyone. It is not wise to waste time explaining yourself to people who will never understand you anyway. Be careful of sharing your heart with people who don't have your best interest at heart. Many dreams are destroyed because they are shared with individuals that are secretly trying to sabotage them instead of solidifying them.

I - **You are Intelligent**. There are many levels of intellect and while we all may not be on the same level, we all have our own individual level of intellect and it is valuable. The best way to increase your intellect is to ask questions and read, especially the fine print. **It is can be very difficult**

to make great decisions with poor information, which is why both of the aforementioned are important. Your level of intelligence is predicated upon your level of commitment. I will provide the blueprint on how to increase in this area in the TTD Principle.

N - Never become so consumed about what people think that you fail to obey the voice of your conscious. This level of action will require you to think in silence rather than thinking out loud. Thinking silently is when you receive instructions that only you and God know about. Thinking out loud invites unwanted distractions and unwanted hate in our lives, simply because we are providing ammunition to associates sent to assassinate our assignment by giving them information they should not have. Be careful of asking those around you what they think because your original purpose will become watered down and you go from following your heart to following their opinion. This will ultimately have you frustrated.

K - Keep quiet. Sometimes you have to make moves in silence because in life there are 3 things that are for certain when it comes to your elevation in life and that is…

(1) Everyone can't handle your transparency

(2) Everyone can't handle your transition and

(3) Everyone can't handle your transformation.

Start thinking for yourself and learn to keep your thoughts to yourself at times. Life is so much better when you take the shackles off of your mind.

A broken pencil still has an eraser and broken crayons can still color. You may have been broken in the past but you still serve a purpose now. Never let the hurt stop you.

~

Wake Your Successful Self Up

9

CELEBRATE YOUR SCARS
THE
"I'M HURT BUT I'M HEALING"
MINDSET

Scars serve as a reminder of what not to do, where not to go and who not to call.

Healing and how you heal is a very touchy subject as there is no cookie cutter way to grieve. The purpose of this chapter is to encourage you not to allow what hurt you to hinder you from moving forward. Healing is indeed a process and although many say that time heals, I have found that time helps but it doesn't guarantee healing. One of the first steps to healing is acknowledging your feelings because pain does not discriminate. **YOU MUST GIVE YOURSELF PERMISSION TO FEEL SO THAT YOU CAN TRULY HEAL.** I've always been a firm believer that it's important to surround yourself with strong friends when you are having weak moments as you embrace your healing. When my mom was murdered as a victim of domestic violence, my perspective on life changed forever. It made me become more legacy focused and aware of how I treat people and how I spend my time. I'm sharing this because someone reading this need to know that no matter what has happened to you or in your past, you cannot let the memory of what happened stop you from moving forward.

NEVER BECOME TOO BUSY TO FEEL

The day my mom was murdered began as a normal day to me. The day was beautiful in the sense that I had the opportunity to speak with her that morning prior to her death about her upcoming trip. The second week in September was always an exciting time for me as my mom always made the annual trip from Michigan to visit family for the Southern Heritage Classic football game in Memphis, Tennessee. That all changed the next day when I received the news that her ex-husband had murdered her a few hours after we spoke. My initial response was shock and it caused a sense of numbness for me. It was my walk with God and faith in God that served as the source of my strength during the initial moments. Although I had quoted Philippians 4:7 which says "And the peace of God, which passeth all understanding, shall keep your hearts and minds through Christ Jesus" many times, that moment was the first time I totally understood it. It was during these moments that I realized what was in me was greater than what was going on around me. During the days and weeks after her death, my primary focus was handling all estate affairs and business related to her homegoing service. The process was longer than normal as my family had to wait on the autopsy and murder investigation to be complete. We then had to coordinate transporting my mother's body from Michigan to Mississippi after it was released to a funeral home hours away from the city in which she was murdered. After flying her body to Mississippi, my family then had to make arrangements with a local funeral home to coordinate the homegoing services.

In all the planning and handling business, the one thing that I was too busy to do was take some time and feel. I never slowed down enough to process my emotions and give myself time to feel the pain so that I could heal properly.

> **YOU MAY BE ABLE TO NUMB YOUR PAIN BUT YOU CAN'T AVOID IT BECAUSE IT WILL SOON RESURFACE.**

DO NOT TAKE IT PERSONAL

My mom's homegoing service was just the first layer of pain that I had to get over. With family member's emotions on high and edge, things that were never said came out as displaced anger. The lesson learned during this second phase of healing for me was understanding that you cannot take anything personal when pain is involved. **Many times people hurt you not because they purpose to, you just happened to be the only and closest thing for them to lash out and project their anger unto.** These things cannot be taken personal.

When you take the pain caused by others personal, you make it about you when it is not about you, which can cause it to become detrimental to your personal relationships. This is why it is important that you find a healthy outlet to lean on. You may have to lean on your faith, your friends and your family. Writing, praying, journaling and counseling helps with ensuring that the feelings of rejection, disappointment and betrayal that caused you pain do not turn into bitterness. The key in this process is to acknowledge that you are indeed hurt but you are healing.

FORGIVENESS IS A PROCESS

Each day you have to make a decision to forgive. You have to choose to think good thoughts and to think the best at all times. Forgiveness is a decision you must make and something that you must practice every day. It will not always be easy but when love is the goal, it will be worthwhile. While there are many types of love, when you are purposed in your heart to forgive, you must strive for the Agape kind of love at all times.

Months after my mom's murder I had to put this into practice. While the wound of her passing was still fresh, I would find myself reliving it all over again as I endured a 15 hour drive along icy roads and 4 inches of snow from Mississippi to Michigan for the sentencing of her murderer. The same man that ask me if he could have my mom's hand in marriage was the same man that used those very hands to take her life. I had this replaying in my mind the entire journey up until the day of the sentencing. Standing only feet away from my mom's murderer, every negative emotion within me was visible and the thoughts of hurting the person that hurt me and my family was all that was on my mind. As these thoughts raced through my mind, I faintly heard the voice of the judge in the background as he asked if the family had anything to say to the accused. The eyes of every armed guard were on me as my entire disposition expressed the anger that was in my heart. As I approached the stand to speak, a calm yet gentle peace came over me as I could hear God say to me crystal clear, **"When you choose not to forgive people here on earth, you forfeit your reservations in heaven.** As my mouth opened, the hate filled words that I had planned to say to my mom's murderer were changed to, "I do not respect you, but I forgive you." Saying those words was hard because it did not reflect how I really felt. Even though I obeyed God, my flesh still wanted to respond. My flesh, my mind and my spirit were all at war with each other. Not only did God speak to me during that brief moment, but I also had a conversation with myself as I tried to remove the death stare from my face. I found myself saying over and over again, "Who in hell is worth you going to hell over?" as I slowly walked back to my seat. What helped me overcome this pain was my faith and obedience to God in the middle of my storm. The pain is still real and recovering from it is a daily task. This one things I know to be true and that is, on the other side of your pain is purpose and on the other side of your pain is healing.

Give yourself time for both to manifest properly and don't rush the process. God will always give you an opportunity to right your wrongs and sometimes cause you to cross paths of those you may have wronged or those that may have wronged you. Forgiveness is a serious matter and being able to walk in instant forgiveness is a measure of your maturity. Understand that forgiveness is a process, especially when you've been hurt really bad. **Just because you forgive them today does not mean you have to do lunch with them tomorrow.**

WAKE YOUR SUCCESSFUL SELF UP™

Forgiveness is mandatory but reconciliation isn't. The most important thing to remember is that we must give ourselves time to heal to the place where we learn how to eventually walk in instant forgiveness. Forgiveness takes practice and practice takes time.

THE PRINCIPLE OF FORGIVENESS

Every one of us has been hurt deeply by someone else. It may have been a parent, an ex-spouse, a current mate, a sibling, an former friend, a relative, or perhaps a stranger. It might be a hurt that came from some violent or reckless act. It may have been something that somebody should have done but didn't. It may be something that took place years ago. Past emotional, mental or physical abuse, or being deeply hurt or mistreated by a friend or a enemy, are common causes of depression. You might have had your share of such experiences. Bitterness, anger and unforgiveness are typical responses to such injustices suffered. The Bible gives us ample instructions on how to overcome them. In many of the above cases, especially where abuse is involved, **getting help from a trained Christian counselor or a professional healthcare worker is highly recommended if not absolutely necessary.**

DON'T DWELL ON THE PAST

Isaiah 43:18-19 says "Forget the former things; do not dwell on the past. See, I am doing a new thing! Now it springs up; do you not perceive it? I am making a way in the desert and streams in the wasteland." This passage provides a vivid description of a life damaged by past hurts – a life that has become a wasteland, a desert. Dwelling upon a record of wrongs weighs us down and heavily burdens us. But the Lord's instructions to forget those former things and not dwell on them, comes with a beautiful promise. Letting them go releases streams of living water into our life and enables God to do a new work in us. One of the greatest new works Christ does in our lives is to bring us to a place where we can forgive those who have hurt us. This is such an important aspect of our daily Christian walk that Jesus included it as part of the prayer found in Luke 11:4 "Forgive us our sins, for we also forgive everyone who sins against us." Instead of dwelling on past hurts, we can let go of those memories and forgive the person that hurt us. Although we cannot make ourselves forget the memories, if you stop clinging to them the painful associations will fade significantly. The ultimate goal when navigating through painful circumstances is to continue to walk in love.

> "Love is patient, love is kind. It does not envy, or does not boast, it is not proud. It is not rude, it is not self-seeking, it is not easily angered, it keeps no record of wrongs." ~ 1 Corinthians 13: 4-5

UNFORGIVENESS IS NOT YOUR IDENTITY

One reason you may have trouble letting go of past hurts might be because they have become part of your identity. "I am this way because of how that person mistreated me," was an excuse some believed. You feared that if you let go of the anger and record of wrongs and forgave the person who hurt you, you would lose a part of yourself and your power. However, Jesus taught us that such fears were unfounded, that we did not have to hold onto past hurts to maintain our identity and power. He showed us that there was another option to allow His love and forgiveness to flow from us towards the person who hurt us. When I did this, instead of anger and the record of past wrongs, Christ's love and forgiveness became part of my identity. When we let Christ's love and forgiveness become part of who we are, we change and become more like him. Our goal is to become more like Him.

> "It is no longer I who live, but Christ lives in me. So I live in this earthly body by trusting in the Son of God, who loved me and gave himself for me." ~ Galatians 2:20 (NLT)

As we learn to surrender our lives to Christ, He can give us such a powerful revelation of His love for us that we can view others through His loving gaze rather than through the lense our pain.

UNFORGIVENESS CAUSES MORE HURT

If we have been deeply hurt by someone in the past, we earnestly desire to flee that pain and be set free from the wounds. A thought you should bear in mind is that by consciously or unconsciously harbouring anger, bitterness, and unforgiveness towards that person, we unwittingly participate in keeping those wounds fresh and unable to heal. That is one reason that Jesus spoke so often of the importance of forgiving those who have wronged us. By not forgiving them, we hurt ourselves even more.

> **If you don't forgive them, sooner or later you're going to start to resemble the people who hurt you. Forgiveness isn't for them, it's for you.**

FORGIVE OTHERS

Forgiveness does not make them right, it makes you free. The most liberating Biblical truth that helps us to forgive those who have treated us unjustly is to recognize the depths to which God has forgiven us. Why does the Bible say, "For if you forgive men when they sin against you, your heavenly Father will also forgive you," Matthew 6:14? It is because for us to refuse to forgive others after God has forgiven our massive debts towards Him, shows a lack of appreciation of how much God has forgiven us. Regardless of how much we have been hurt by others, forgive them as you apply the **I'm hurt but I'm healing mindset**. If God forgives us of our numerous sins towards Him, we can forgive others of their sin.

> "But love your enemies, do good to them, and lend to them without expecting to get anything back. Then your reward will be great, and you will be sons of the Most High…Be merciful, just as your Father is merciful." ~ Luke 6:35-36 (NIV)

Forgiveness is often an act of faith. Don't wait on a feeling to forgive people because you may never feel like forgiving them. Deal with your feelings later, but forgive them now so that you can move on from that situation.

FORGIVE THEM AND FORGIVE YOURSELF

FORGIVENESS LETTER

To every person that mistreated me and abused my love, I forgive you.

To every person that caused me pain and made me doubt how great I was born to be, I forgive you.

To every person that lied to me, I forgive you.

To every person that rejected me and told me NO, I want to say Thank you for expelling yourself out of my life when I was too blind to see that you weren't part of my purpose. Thank you for helping me not waste my time on you and with you.

I FORGIVE YOU!

A broken pencil still has an eraser and broken crayons can still color. You may have been broken in the past but you still serve a purpose now. Never let the hurt stop you.

~

Wake Your Successful Self Up

10

IT'S OKAY TO BE SELFISH
THE
"SELF SERVING"
MINDSET

"Sometimes you have to be selfish to be selfless."
~ Edward Albert

Better is always available. If you're married you can become a better spouse. If you have children you can become a better parent. If you are single, you can become a better you so that when you find your partner of purpose, you can have a clear focus of who you are and not get lost in who they want you to be. The foundation to serving others well is first learning how to serve yourself well. This always begins with the "SELF SERVING" Mindset not the SELF centered mindset. We are often taught not to be selfish. Growing up many of us were taught the importance of sharing and giving. We were often told repeatedly not to be selfish. This type of thinking somehow penetrated the perimeters of your adulthood leaving us vulnerable for unhealthy boundaries. We make or have made the mistake of giving our time, energy, resources and love to people who are selfish in their motives.

After expending the aforementioned, we set ourselves up for failure leaving us full of regret and bitterness. Many fall into guilt when people say to them, "don't be selfish." The "don't be selfish" mindset is unhealthy. You must at some point in your life learn to be selfish. If you do not take the time to take care of you then how will you be able to take care of others? Perhaps you are reading these words and you are considering leaving that job or relationship and you're worried about whether or not they will say you are selfish for leaving. Do not allow the guilt to keep you bound. The same people that are saying that you are selfish for leaving are selfish for wanting you to stay. At the end of the day, sometimes you have to be selfish and the decisions you make in life are not for everyone to like, they are for you to live with. When it comes to your sanity and your purpose, sometimes you have to be selfish.

DATE YOURSELF EXERCISE

When you give and pour out a lot, you must also take some time to replenish. You cannot make saying yes to everyone else and no to yourself part of your everyday regimen. At some point you must call a timeout and take some time to rejuvenate. It's not call quitting, it's call resting. The best way to serve yourself is to date yourself. I recommend selecting the one day that works for your schedule where you can go for an hour or two uninterrupted. This can be at a park, at your favorite restaurant, or coffee shop. The key to dating yourself is to make sure that you are in a place where you can have a moment of stillness and take notes. The notes you will be taking will be to analyze how you can better serve yourself and those around you. Here are three questions to ask yourself when dating yourself. (1) How Can I Better? (2) Can I Love A Little Harder (3) Who Can I Be Blessing To? Write down three things pertaining to each question that you can improve immediately in all three areas and implement them as soon as you are able.

VALUE YOUR PEACE

Peace is found when you begin to release everything that is not adding value to your life. No one can do it for you, give it to you, find it for you or buy it for you but YOU. Know that you are loved and that you are valuable. Do not be too hard on yourself or feel unworthy of whatever you have. Time should not be wasted beating yourself up over temporary setbacks or simple mistakes you have made. Never beat yourself up for what you have done wrong, always build yourself up for what you are doing right. Remember that failure is the best learning opportunity there is because it generates growth. Do not live in the past, it usually leads to stagnation, disappointment and regrets. Learn to speak up for yourself and never allow people to treat you poorly. Constantly putting yourself down hinders any development you desire to make, so knowing and emphasizing your value is a step in the right direction.

YOU DESERVE TO BE HAPPY

If you let them walk all over you because you are afraid of losing them, you lose yourself in the process. It is okay to be selfish sometimes because in doing so, you always add value to yourself. Know your worth and add interest to it as other people's perception of you is not your reality; it is what you think of yourself that matters most. Concentrate on your successes rather than your failures, although you should look into your failures and learn from the reasons you failed.

"You can't please, fix, help or love people until you fix, help and love yourself. Self awareness is not selfishness"

~

Pastor Hart Ramsey

11

LOVE YOURSELF ENOUGH TO SAY NO

Everything and everyone shouldn't have your attention. Create balance in your life by saying "NO" to anything and anyone not in alignment with your purpose.

During this self care journey, one of the most important words you will need to incorporate in your vocabulary is NO. Understand that people can only misuse and mistreat you with your permission. Your inability to say no comes at a price. Choosing to say yes at the expense of your peace is not healthy. Choosing to say yes at the pleasure of receiving validation and affirmation for egotistical purposes is not healthy. Accept who and what you are, make changes to yourself that you feel are necessary instead of what someone else thinks is necessary. There will be times where compromise is essential but it should never come at the expense of you devaluing yourself. Using the word no effectively and appropriately will not only save you time, but it will save heartache and money as well. What and who are you saying yes to that you need and should have given a simple No? Are you making excuses for the things and people that are draining you as opposed to giving you life? Are you making excuses for the habits and people you need to be excusing out of your life?

YOU HAVE "NO EXCUSE" EXERCISE

1. Write down 7 Excuses you have made that have caused you to remain stagnant. If you do not have 7 that is okay. This exercise is designed to help you detox and eliminate all excuses and reasons you have told yourself NO and said yes to things and people that are not healthy for you. Do not speak these excuses or reasons out verbally as you must choose the words you put out in the atmosphere carefully. You are to simply write these down.

2. Write down the antidote to these excuses. The antidote is your solution to the written excuses. Unlike your excuses, these antidotes are to be spoken verbally. These antidotes are to be words of life that will counteract every excuse written.

3. Write down 7 unhealthy thoughts or habits you have said yes to that you should have said No to this month. Again, do not speak these things, write them down.

4. Write down your Antidotes to the 7 Yeses you have given to those unhealthy thoughts and habits. You may not have 7 so write all that apply. These antidotes are to be spoken as this will be critical in creating healthy thoughts and habits. Give yourself time to see the results you desire. Repetition is the mother to excellence and consistency is the key to your breakthrough. Practice these exercises as often as needed and practice saying no to everything antithetical to your growth. Growth comes when you stay connected to people that won't allow you to make excuses. Stop making excuses for the things and people you need to be excusing out of your life. Practicing the exercises above will help you gauge when it's time for their exit or your exit. As it relates to your exit, do not try to explain it. When it's time to go, it is time to go and you do not owe anyone an explanation. If you do not have peace about a business deal, environment or relationship, let your exit be in silence and be swift. Exit without Explanation and choose to say no to anything unhealthy to your growth and yes to yourself!!! It's not people's place to approve for you what God has assigned to you, it's their place to confirm what has already been spoken. Get advice from people but don't let the advice you get become louder than the instructions you got from God.

"It's either black or white, good or bad, successful or unsuccessful, Yes or No...there is no in between"

~

Cleophas Kinnel, III

12

CONSISTENCY IS THE KEY TO YOUR BREAKTHROUGH
THE
"TTD PRINCIPLE"
OF BEING DISCIPLINED

Waking Your Successful Self requires consistency and discipline. This comes when you develop healthy habits and make the decision to destroy "The Average" Mindset. Author Roderick Richardson has one of the most profound quotes I've ever heard in life. As a matter of fact, I've adopted this particular quote as one of my personal mantras in life for operating in excellence. Richardson simply says, "Good is alright but if better is out there then good is not enough." It reminds me that just because you are content in your situation does not mean you are to be content with your situation. I remember one day after my normal workout routine, I came home flexing and looking in the mirror and my wife said to me, "Baby you look good, but never get satisfied. When you are thirsty for success and greatness, you must never become satisfied with being average or the status quo." This is what makes great companies and great people great. They never become married to average and they are always in pursuit of becoming a better version of themselves.

As I lay out this principle, I have a few questions to ask you.

(1) How committed are you to gaining more wisdom and knowledge in the areas of life you need to Wake Your Successful Self Up?

(2) How committed are you to better managing your time, your energy and your craft?

(3) How committed are you to becoming a Better Version of You?

The more we engage and do things no matter what it is, we become better and eventually enter the arena of mastery. As I lay out these principles, you will need to keep these words in mind...

CONSISTENCY MAKES THE HARD THINGS IN LIFE EASY.

The TTD Principle was birth during my transition as a pescetarian. I haven't always been a health enthusiast, but after spending several years working for the Jackson Heart Study as one of the initial Research Recruiters, I began to see how poor diet played a major part in the lives of others. It wasn't until my wife and I got food poisoned that I made the complete change in my dietary preference. Even though I wanted to change, the change never came. The food poisoning generated that change and made me realize that sometimes we don't change until we are pushed in a corner and forced to change. That change birthed the principle that is partially responsible for this book.

What is the TTD Principle?

The TTD Principle is a systematic format that enables you to better manage all areas of your life. The letters stand for **Track The Day, Track The Diet** and **Track The Dollar**. Everything in our lives can be placed in one of these categories. From your profession to your finances, it all can be placed here.

TRACK THE DAY

Your time is valuable so don't allow people who don't value your time to waste it. Just because people are negligent with their time doesn't mean that you should give them permission to be negligent with yours. The people, places and things in our lives will either cause us to be better or bitter, prosperous or poor. Your time will be the barometer on how those you come in contact with value you. Time is one of the most precious commodities you have while you are here on earth and if the people in your life do not respect your time, then they in essence do not respect you. The minute you give people permission to mismanage your time, is the minute you give people the power to control your life. Your life is composed up of nothing but time and numbers. We are born at a certain date and we will leave this earth at a certain day and time. What we decide to do with the minutes, hours, days, months and years in between is our responsibility. Tracking Your Day is knowing how to become a better steward of your time and knowing how to value it properly. Are the people around you causing you to appreciate in value or depreciate in value when it comes to your time? Who or what is hindering you from being a better steward of your time? Take some time to think about these things so that you can take back control of your time if you are placing it in the hands of someone negligent.

Tracking the day is the component of this principle that will help you better serve yourself and those around you. I've come to find out that our lives are composed up of time and numbers and everything we do and love revolves around time and numbers or what some might call (ROI) return on investment. Sporting teams give their personnel, coaches and players a certain amount of numbers (dollars) with the expectation that they will produce a certain amount of numbers (Wins and Stats) within a certain amount of time. If the numbers are not produced within the expected time, the teams seek someone that will produce the desired results. Our parents spent a certain amount of time with each other to produce us and we came out at a certain date and time, weighing a certain number. Even when your assignment here on earth is complete, you will be remembered by three things.

The time you arrived here on earth, the accomplishments you achieved during your time on earth, and the time you are assigned to leave this earth. For this very reason, you must become more aware of who you spend your time with, what you spend your time doing, where you spend your time and how you spend your time. You will be challenged shortly to Wake Your Successful Self Up in this area if you aren't already awake!

I often share with others on how I wake up at 4:30 a.m. each morning like clockwork and how I run daily and the usual response I receive is, "I don't have time." I'm here to tell you that you always have time to do what is a priority to you. I'm here to tell you that you can do it if you properly master your time well. You must have a time mastery mindset and not a time management mindset while using this principle. **You must assign every task of your day to every minute of your day. Everything you do must be with purpose and on purpose during this process.** Your workday time may vary depending on your occupation but these principles will still work for you if you work them.

---

3 A's to Tracking Your Day

Assign: Assign Each Task To A Time

Assist: Determine Who and What Can Assist You

Attack: Attack the Assignment Until Complete

WHAT TIME DO YOU WAKE UP?

I challenge you to wake up 1 hour prior to your normal time with 4:00 a.m. being the earliest starting point. If you already wake at this hour then you are on track with this principle. Next, break down everything you would like to do before you leave the house into 30-minute increments. For example, I wake up at 4:30 a.m. each morning. From 4:30 a.m. to 5:00 a.m. I am having a moment of meditation and prayer. From 5:00 a.m. until 6:00 a.m. I am in the gym working out or out running. From 6:00 a.m. - 7:00 a.m. I am getting prepared for the office and my children ready for their day. This may not work for you but I am sharing this as a starting point to illustrate how much can be done before most people awake and to share why waking early is an important part of success.

There will be times when life will happen and things will not be in your control. In moments like these, it will be easy to shift mentally once you have developed the pattern of rising early physically and preparing properly.

TRACK THE DIET

Tracking the diet is the foundation to this principle. By diet I am not only referencing what you eat physically but also what you digest spiritually and mentally. You must safeguard your heart and not allow anything or anyone to contaminate it. Your diet is the one thing that will determine how well your day goes and your diet will determine the longevity of your dollar. When I became a pescetarian, I became frustrated when I initially began to eat out.

Since I do not eat chicken, pork or beef, finding an establishment to cater to my dietary preference was challenging. This forced me to become more diligent with planning and preparing meals for my family. This has also made me realize that almost everything in fast food is chicken, pork and beef and it caused me not to eat out as much, which saved me money. Monitoring your diet from all areas of life is important. As mentioned earlier, you cannot make great decisions with poor information. This is why your mental diet must be fed by reading or listening to things that will give you life.

The same applies to your spiritual life. You must replace that which is negative in your life with something positive so that you can maintain a healthy balance in life. What good is it for you to be strong spiritually if you are too sick to carry out the assignment given to you? Tracking Your Day and Tracking Your Diet will bring balance to the deficiencies in these areas. A healthy lifestyles comes when you monitor your diet in all areas of life.

TRACK THE DOLLAR

Tracking the Dollar is about discipline and learning to stay in your financial lane. It's about not going broke trying to impress other broke people. Do you know where your money is going? Do you know exactly what you are spending your money on? If someone were to walk up to you and say they wanted to pay off your debt, do you know how much you owe? Do you need the cable, clothes and cars or can you go a season without them in order to finance your dreams and build a legacy for those around you? I have heard people say that they need more money and some do, but money mastery must proceed this or the chase for money will continue.

A millionaire mentor of mine once told me to stop thinking about money. He said, "Money and the use of it comes with wisdom and understanding. The wise are rich and more of anything just naturally comes, including money, if that's their desire. The foolish are poor, and blessings, including money naturally elude them. Don't pursue money. Seek understanding and wisdom and all else will naturally flow."

Tracking the Dollar is also about generating positive energy in your life and keeping your dollar circulating. When you track the dollar in your mind, you must imagine your dollar growing and finding its way back to you or it will never arrive. The law of vision says that if you can't see it, you can't have it and this holds true with this principle. You must place the dollar in areas of growth so that it can produce for you and those around you.

This can be accomplished by applying the S.O.S. component of this principle. S.O.S. means that you should either sow or sale all non-essentials in your life. Selling provides an opportunity for you to regain money spent on things that you wanted but didn't really need. Sowing provides the opportunity for you to circulate your dollar in the universe thus creating a great chance for you to receive a return on that which was sown. This hold true not just for your dollar, but for your time, energy and love as well.

> *"Give, and it will be given to you. They will pour into your lap a good measure – pressed down, shaken together, and running over. For by your standard of measure it will be measured to you in return ~ Luke 6:38 (NASB)*

Either the things in your life are beneficial or they are detrimental and this principle provides you the opportunity to identify that. I challenge you to Track Your Dollar so that is can better serve you and mankind for the greater good.

Success is expensive. It's going to cost you friendships, time, sleep and money. If you're not willing to pay, you might as well get comfortable being mediocre.

~

Wake Your Successful Self Up

13

THE
"GOOD GOD I'M GREAT"
MINDSET

"You are from God, little children, and have overcome them; because greater is He who is in you than he who is in the world." ~ I John 4:4

The Good God I'm Great principle is about developing a mindset of healthy self-esteem. Many times life will happen and you won't always feel your best and this mindset will be the fuel that will keep the fire within you burning. Practicing this principle will help you stay sharp and maintain your identity. When you view yourself in the way God created you, you will begin to do what you were created to do and that is to be creative. Your inner perception will determine your outward reflection, which will determine how others perceive you.

When this perception is healthy, you will draw both love and hate. When you know who you are and others have yet to identify who they are within, they will perceive you as thinking you are better than them when in reality, you just know who you are. These individuals will often show their inner perception of you in the form of insecurity, jealousy and hatred. Do not allow this in any way make you think that anything is wrong with you. Never compromise who you are because others do not know who they are. Your inner love must overcome all of the above. You must allow the love within you to overcome all that oppose your Good God I'm Great mindset. This principle will require daily adjustment. You must always view yourself as being great. Not with a sense of arrogance but with a sense of confidence. People that will only recognize your old identity do not belong in your new season.

Don't think it strange when people who used to know you mistake you for being the person you used to be. Do not take offense to this as they do not mean any harm. They simply have mistaken identity and need an update and it is your responsibility to share who you've become to them.

You have to develop a palate for greatness or you will forever be eating from the table of mediocrity. The question is never if you want it, the question is always HOW BAD DO YOU WANT IT? Purpose in your heart to Grow Gracefully and Change Constantly. You can't make epic moves doing business with a mediocre mindset. You must make it your purpose to surround yourself with individuals who are strong in the areas in which you need improvement. Always remember that "Iron sharpens iron but you can't be sharp hanging around butter knife people." You can't expect to fly with the eagles with a chicken mindset. This is why being around those who are smarter is so important. They will sharpen you to the place where you will become stronger, wiser and better.

SOUND THE ALARM

It's time for you to WAKE YOUR SUCCESSFUL SELF UP and live your dreams. It's time for you to WAKE YOUR SUCCESSFUL SELF UP and be who and what you are purposed to be.
Stop seeking permission from people to be great. God created you in His image and likeness so greatness is in your blood. Don't limit yourself and don't sleep on your potential. You are destined for greatness. Greatness is on the inside of you and your next level is right around the corner.

To everyone at Team Wake Your Successful Self Up, thank you for supporting this work. Thanks to those of you that shared your motivational words with me. They served as my source of inspiration and I could not complete this book without your words being a part of it.

FAITH – (Flow In It) (JERMEL LILLY)
CONSISTENT (Stay In It) (JEFF KARLIN)
CONFIDENCE – (Walk In It) MARY JOHNSON
STRIVE – (Press Toward It) ELAINE PINDER
UNSTOPPABLE – (You Are This) DAUREN FRANCIS
HOPE – (Maintain It) SANDRA SIMPSON
LIFE – (Enjoy It) CATHERINE PETERSON
BE ENCOURAGED – (Always) (SHAYLA HOLMES
PURPOSE – (Get To Know It) ERICA LEE
KOBE – (Master Your Craft) NYSHEKA WARE
VALUABLE – (Know Your Worth) LATRICE LYDE
Guardian REDEEMER – (Trust God) KRISTA WATSON
SOULS – (Serve Others Well) SHILA CASEY

As you embrace this journey, keep these words and the following acronyms in mind and allow them to be your source of inspiration and motivation.

THIS IS ONLY A T.E.S.T

T - **Tests** are not designed to destroy you. Tests are only designed to test you and not take you out. Whatever it is that you are going through right now will pass.

E – **Examination and Exfoliation** Tests come to examine what is on the inside on you. Many of the hardships you face in life will show you what you are made of, who is for you and who is against you. Exams show you what you know and help to remove the excess in your life. Your **examinations will always create an exfoliation**. Whatever and whoever is attached to you that is not suppose to be attached to you will be realized during your times of testing.

S – **Stronger** When your test is complete, you will be wiser, better and above all you will be stronger.

T– **Take some time to rest and recover** Whenever you are being tested, make sure you take some time to rest and recover. If you do not slow down and get some rest, your body will shut down and make you rest. You cannot keep pressing through pain as part of your everyday regimen. At some point you must call a timeout and take some time and rest.

The 3 S's To Expect When You Wake Your Successful Self Up

1. Expect a SITUATION to happen that will help catapult you to your next level.

2. Maintain a level of SERIOUSNESS and laser focus to help you with your next level.

3. Expect to have a SOLUTION to the opportunities presented to you as you reach your next level.

F.O.C.U.S.

F – Fix your eyes on your destination not your location.

O – Do not be easily offended. Everyone will not support your purpose or your dreams so do not be alarmed.

C – Do not cause unnecessary damage by speaking words that are detrimental to your mission. Do not let your mouth murder your miracle.

U – Understand that everyone is not going to understand your purpose and it is not your responsibility to make it.

S – See beyond what you see. The law of vision says that if you can't see it then you can't have it. Once you capture it in your mind and act on what you see, anything is possible.

<u>CTRL + ALT + DELETE</u>
LESSONS FROM THE KEYBOARD

Do not be deceived. Everyone that is smiling at you is not happy for you. There will be those that will call you crazy for believing in your dreams and those that will try to make you abort your dreams. Don't fight the separations that are happening in your life right now. Holding on to people that clearly need to be out of your life is sabotage to your future. Much like a computer, when it's time to restart and reset, pressing CTRL + ALT+ DELETE is the method that is used. So it is in life.

Anything that tries to **CTRL (Control)** your life and **ALT (Alter)** your purpose needed to be **DELETED** our of your life so that you can fulfill your purpose.

P.U.S.H.

P – Push past petty.

In order for you to push into your purpose you will have to push past petty things and petty people.

U – Uncomfortable and Unpopular.

You will then have to do that which is uncomfortable and that which is unpopular.

S – Soreness then soaring.

To experience the growth you desire, you will have to go through a season of soreness before you go through a season of soaring.

H – How In The World.

When you are pushing and giving birth to your purpose, you may wonder how in the world it will come to fruition. Focus on the finish line and know that it will happened when it is purposed to happen.

ABOUT THE AUTHOR

Felix Anderson is an Author, Brand Advocate, Speaker, Life Catalyst and Founder/CEO of The Executive Concierges. With over 20 years of customer service experience, the passion to serve others and to help them understand the core principles of customer service has always been at the forefront. After his mother was murdered at the hands of domestic violence, he become a voice for the voiceless and was selected as a 2014 Man of Character for his role in helping fight domestic violence. He is a health enthusiast and leader that possess an undeniable energy and practical wisdom distinctiveness like no other with the mission to teach you how to better serve yourself and those around you.

Made in the USA
Columbia, SC
27 August 2020

17509105R00074